Blessed Imelda Lambertini

Patroness of First Communicants

Featuring the artwork of Caroline Spinelli

"Blessed is the man who endures trial, for when he has stood the test he will receive the crown of life which God has promised to those who love Him."
James 1:12

HELPING YOU BRING THE JOY OF THE FAITH TO YOUR FAMILY

We bring you and your family inspiring stories that have motivated children (and adults) from the dawn of the Christian era: the true-life stories of people just like you who lived their lives "striving to win the heavenly crown"!

Check out all of our products online at **www.HolyHeroes.com**

The "Life of Jesus" Coloring Books

Featuring artwork from the following illustrators:
Enoc Castaneda, Chris Pelicano, Caroline Spinelli, and John Webber

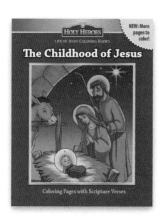  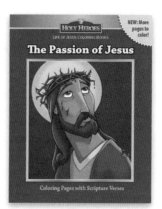 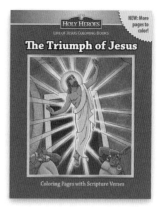

Get more FREE coloring and activity pages online at
www.HolyHeroesFun.com

ISBN 978-1-936330-04-1   ©2020 Holy Heroes LLC. All rights reserved. Printed in the U.S.A. (Keys/RRD)

Imelda Lambertini was born in Bologna, Italy in 1322. She was the beloved only child of a wealthy couple. Her family was very devout. They attended Mass together often.

Imelda's mother often let Imelda help her bring food and clothing to the poor people of their town. One day, Imelda asked, "Why do we have to feed the poor? Why doesn't Jesus simply give all the poor people food so they won't be hungry anymore?"

Her mother smiled. "Jesus always cares for the poor. Remember when Jesus fed
all the people on the hillside with just a few fishes and loaves of bread?
Jesus blessed the bread, then told His Apostles to give it to the people.
What looked like very few loaves of bread miraculously fed everyone their fill."

Imelda gave an impish grin, "I wish I could have asked the Apostles for some of that bread. I'm sure it tasted better than any ordinary bread—but your bread tastes good, too, Mama."

"Thank you, my little one. But the people who ate the bread grew hungry later on,
so they came to Jesus the next day for more miraculous bread.
But Jesus surprised them by promising them a different bread, the Bread of
Eternal Life, which would give them life forever in Heaven."

"That sounds even better. Did He give them that bread?" Imelda asked. "No, not right then," explained her mother. "But Jesus did tell them that this special Bread that would give Eternal Life was...His Own Body." Imelda was puzzled. "Mama, how can Jesus give us His Body to eat?"

Her mother explained, "Jesus is God, and He needs only to speak a word to make it so. Many times during His life, Jesus did exactly this to help his followers believe in the power of His words. When He said 'Be healed', sick people were well again. When He said 'Be still', the wild waves were calmed on the Sea of Galilee. When He said 'Get up', even the dead came back to life!"

At last, Imelda understood. "I see, Mother! At the Last Supper when Jesus said, 'This is My Body,' the bread truly became His Body and was no longer ordinary bread at all! Oh, Mama! Now I want to eat the Body of Jesus, too! But Jesus lived so long ago. Surely the Bread of Life is gone by now!"

Her mother smiled. "Jesus thought of that, too. He gave the Apostles His own power to make ordinary bread truly His Body. Later, His Apostles passed this power on to new bishops and priests. Today, we can hear our parish priest say, 'This is My Body,' and know they are the words of Jesus making His Own Body truly present to us, even though it still looks like bread."

Imelda's eyes sparkled. "Jesus takes such good care of us! I want to go to Mass every day to hear the priest say, 'This is My Body' and know that Jesus is really there on the altar! Oh, Mother, most of all I want to be fed with the Body of Jesus in Holy Communion!"

"Then Jesus is feeding the poor, and everyone!" cried little Imelda. "Yes, through His priests He feeds them Bread from Heaven, but He still expects us to feed the poor like He did on earth, by sharing our food and other blessings with them as we can," her mother added.

From that time on, Imelda had a special love for Jesus in the Blessed Sacrament and longed to receive Him at every Mass. At that time, however, children could not receive their first Holy Communion until age fourteen, so the five-year-old Imelda tried to be patient until that far-off day.

When Imelda was nine years old, she asked permission to enter the Dominican convent in Val di Pietra and live with the nuns there. It was not unusual at that time for girls to enter a convent or marry at a very young age. Although her parents knew they would miss their little daughter, they gave her to God willingly.

The nuns taught Imelda all about living a life in service to God. She wore the Dominican habit and participated as much as she was allowed in the life of the convent. The nuns knew Imelda longed to make her First Communion early, but the prioress and the priest told her she would have to wait a few more years.

Imelda prayed earnestly to Jesus to grant her desire to receive Him sooner than the age of 14.
As she watched the nuns prepare for Communion, she thought, "How can anyone receive Our Lord and not die of happiness?" At every Mass she waited hopefully for any sign that she would be allowed to approach the altar.

But at every Mass, while the other nuns made their thanksgiving after Communion, Imelda suffered her disappointment silently. She redoubled her plea, "Please, come to me, my Jesus, for I am poor and without the bread I need to live. Please let me receive You into my heart in Holy Communion!"

In May of 1333, when she was 11 years old, Imelda felt a stir of hope and grace in her heart. In her night prayers
on the eve of the Feast of the Ascension, she felt certain Jesus would grant her fondest desire.
As the sisters prepared for the Mass, she asked the priest, "May I receive my First Communion today?"
"No, my child," he replied, "You are still too young."

After Mass, Imelda hid her disappointment and remained in prayer before Jesus in the tabernacle, reminding herself that He said, "Knock and it shall be opened to you, seek and you shall find." "Oh, my Jesus," she prayed, "if I could fly to the tabernacle, I would knock and knock until you would open up and come to me!"

"Oh, my Jesus, I know you are the Bread of Life truly present here in the tabernacle.
You once said, 'Let the children come to Me, and do not hinder them.' I love You
and want so much to come to You, Lord, but my age has stopped me!
I can't reach You, Jesus; will You not come to me Yourself?"

One sister had stayed behind to tidy the chapel after Mass. Hearing a soft sound, she turned toward Imelda and gasped. A great miracle was happening! Jesus in the Blessed Sacrament had come out of the tabernacle and hovered in a glorious light above Imelda's head!

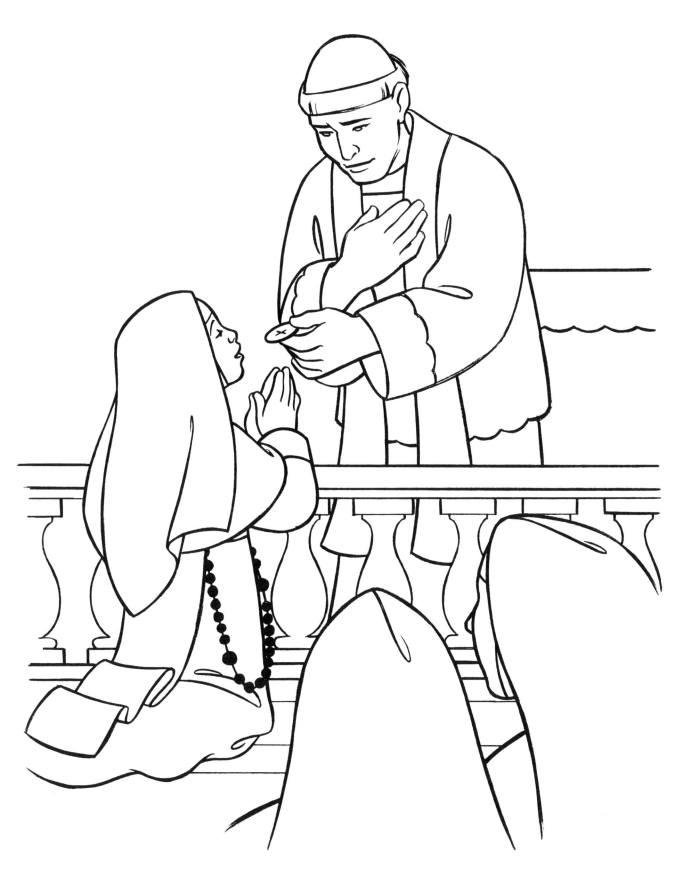

The amazed sister ran to get the priest. He rushed into the chapel, with the whole community at his heels.
He had no doubt what the miracle meant. Reverently, the priest took the shining host and gave the
little Dominican what Jesus Himself had miraculously ordained: her First Holy Communion at the age of eleven.

After a period of thanksgiving, the Prioress guided everyone out of the chapel so Sister Imelda could pray undisturbed. "Leave her alone with Christ in her heart, my sisters," she said. "And let us all thank God for this wonderful grace!"

Imelda remained in the chapel until two sisters came to get her some hours later.
They found Sister Imelda still kneeling at her place. When they touched her shoulder, Imelda collapsed,
still with a beautiful smile on her lips. She had died of happiness—Jesus had come into Imelda's heart
and then taken her to be close to His Heart forever in Heaven!

Blessed Imelda continues to pray for all First Communicants as she looks down
from Heaven where she is so happy. In 1910, Pope St Pius X lowered the age
for First Communion, so now children can receive when they are about seven years old.
He also named Blessed Imelda the Patroness of First Communicants.

Remember that Jesus comes to you in every Mass when the priest says,
"Take this, all of you, and eat of it, for this is My Body, which will be given up for you."

Behold the Lamb of God, behold Him who takes away the sins of the world.
Blessed are those called to the supper of the Lamb.

Blessed Imelda, pray for us!

O Holy Angel, at my side,
Go to the church for me,
Kneel in my place, at Holy Mass
Where I desire to be.

At Offertory, in my stead,
Take all I am and own,
And place it as a sacrifice
Upon the Altar Throne.

At Holy Consecration's bell,
Adore with the Seraph's love,
My Jesus, hidden in the Host,
Come down from Heaven above.

And when the priest Communion takes,
Oh, bring my Lord to me,
That His sweet Heart may rest on mine,
And I His temple be.

Send Your Angel to
HOLY MASS

GLORY STORIES®

A Holy Heroes Production

Saint Elizabeth Ann Seton

"Be Children of the Church!"

You will also enjoy this coloring book! Available at HolyHeroes.com

Saint Faustina and Divine Mercy

Jesus, I trust in You!

Jezu Ufam Tobie

You will also enjoy this coloring book! Available at HolyHeroes.com